Wel

I am so happy that you are here! If you are here- it means that we are kindred spirits. Something about my book drew you in.

Maybe you heard it from someone or saw it somewhere and did a double take and thought, "hmm, I should buy that."

Who knows how you ended up here! All we know is that you're here! That means that something that I share, will do something for you. It could spark anything!

That is magic.

You can spark it too! And that is all I have ever wanted. To show the world- that they can spark too. <3

Do you know why this speaks so loudly to my soul?

Because if something that I share, does something for you, there is a REALLY good chance you are going to do something with it. Maybe you heal something. Maybe you feel less alone. Maybe you feel inspired to share something that inspires someone else. Maybe you make someone feel less alone or share my words with them.

The only outcome that I can see— is you using this in some way shape or form. Even if I spark hot spots for you- that will make you aware of something. And what if you love it!?

That right there does it all for me. That right there is what makes me know that I need to put this out into the world.

What. If. You. Love. It?

I feel melty just thinking about someone connecting with this and finding more of themselves in this story. If I can spark inspiration- or encourage you to share more of who you are with the world -that is beautiful. That makes it all worth it.

I have always wanted to be the little spark. I want to start the fire- watch it spread and then I fizzle off. Rest. Then start something new. I have so much creative energy and I thrive on spreading positivity.

I will never get tired of telling people things that I love about them.

I will never get tired of showing up and changing the energy of a room. I love giving people hope. I love showing people that they already have everything that they need to live their best lives- to feel their most happy- their most peace.

This book – this is the first part of the science experiment. I have always wanted to do it- so I am diving in. I am done getting in my own way. I am done doubting. I am done with all of the negative things I used to do. I am healing. I am thriving.

I am here in this world to help as many people as possible find themselves because, right now, life is good. The more people that are able to find their tools, find themselves and use their uniqueness to create more color in this world, the better the world gets.

And that, my friends, is how we change the world.

Today, before Marco and I had our talk, I was having an angry day. I don't have angry days. But lately I've been healing a big source of my trauma.

I really didn't even realize how many different traumas connected to this one area until I started getting angry. Every single day, for like a week- I would say to Marco- "You know what else I want to say when I think about that guy?"

I'd launch into a story about him, which would connect to something else and just for a few seconds- I was even more enraged.

Every single story would end up with me yelling-

"FUCK THAT GUY!"

And that's when it all hit me.

I was releasing a lot of it.

I felt lighter. I realized that I wasn't so upset anymore. And that got me thinking.

It got me thinking about how this all started. This part of my life has been a whirlwind. Almost 1 year ago – my life changed.

Everything changed. I was catapulted into a world of growth and suddenly, I couldn't go backwards anymore. And let me tell you- I was pretty great at going backwards.

To relationships, to jobs, to anywhere that felt familiar. But now... now I could never see the world how I used to. I could never live the way I used to.

I have so much to give to this world. I share this in hopes that at least one of these short – yet mighty – stories, influence you to do something good, to shake something up or shake something out of your life. To let go of something- to try something- to change something- to just do something- ANYTHING.

And that's when it all hit me.

I was releasing a lot of it.

I felt lighter. I realized that I wasn't so upset anymore. And that got me thinking.

It got me thinking about how this all started.

This part of my life has been a whirlwind. Almost 1 year ago – my life changed.

Everything changed. I was catapulted into a world of growth and suddenly, I couldn't go backwards anymore. And let me tell you- I was pretty great at going backwards.

To relationships, to jobs, to anywhere that felt familiar. But now... now I could never see the world how I used to. I could never live the way I used to.

I have so much to give to this world. I share this in hopes that at least one of these short – yet mighty – stories, influence you to do something good, to shake something up or shake something out of your life. To let go of something- to try something- to change something- to just do something- ANYTHING.

I hope that in reading this, you feel something that sparks you, or is a vibey spot in your day- leads you somewhere new. I hope that it gives you hope – gives you proof, gives you whatever it is you need to believe- that life can still be good, even when it feels messy.

There is a lesson in everything. The sooner we shift our focus off the things that are wrong and into what we gain– the better we recover. The faster things move. The more our lives fill with purpose. The more fulfillment we feel.
And it might not look anything like you pictured.

And that is okay because, I know. I am living proof that you will love it even more than you ever could have dreamed. That anything is possible.

Nothing will ever be perfect- but that doesn't mean it can't still always be wonderful.

The Accident

How many jobs have I worked in my life? I honestly couldn't even tell you. I'd really have to do some research for that, but I won't bore either of us. Let's just say I've worked many jobs in my life.

I've always worked multiple jobs. If it sounded like something I could do – I did it. The customer service industry had A LOT that I could do. And I made it through working three jobs at a time for the majority of my life.

That weighs on you after a while. It made 10 years feel like forty. I was exhausted and, while I was managing- I wasn't making it. I wasn't making enough to really live the life that I wanted. I was burning out. I was losing myself.

After I had my son, I wanted more stability and less of the night life that comes with the industry. When I got an offer to work for a virtual assistant company, it was a no brainer for me. I was going to make more money than I had ever made in my life. Promotions, leveling up- guaranteed advancement. I was stoked!

I worked there for a year. That year I worked my ass off. I worked harder than I ever had. I had time for three jobs before this! Managing one was going to be no problem. I was prepared for this! I prepped my whole life for this. I took on any extra shifts that I possibly could- because, well, I was working from home. I could do everything!

Except, I couldn't do everything.

My son needed me. My life needed me.

I was working 12-18 hours a day. At the time though, it felt like it was great. My checks were going to be INCREDIBLE! I was really showing my value. I was really going to be seen for my worth. I was going to get the validation I had been seeking since I started working, in real net value.

I felt amazing.

On fire.

Nothing could stop me.

And then I got paid.

The checks were not what I was promised. Not even close to what I was promised.

I called my bosses to let them know that my check was all wrong. Obviously, accounting had it wrong, and I wanted to know how to fix it. I thought it'd be an easy fix.

They explained to me that the money would be there, but right now we were working hard to really launch the business. It was still in the process of getting its wings. They needed me. I was crucial to helping them build this.

It would all pay off. They promised. This was guaranteed.

I would be rewarded for all of my efforts. They told me how much they appreciated me and knew that we would be a huge success.

I just needed to hang in a little bit longer.

I agreed.

I was all in.

I am loyal.

I am a hard worker.

I could really help them build this.

We would do this together.

They promoted me right then and there and even promised me more money once we took off.

I was so excited for the financial stability that was coming. I couldn't wait to feel free from the burden of living paycheck to paycheck.

Months went by with no change. People started quitting. My favorite co- worker called me and told me that she was leaving too. She was taking another job. The bosses were starting to unwind. The money was not coming. It went from paying us a little to not paying us at all.

But they kept promising it would all pay off. We just had to trust them.

I wanted to trust them. But- I also had bills due.

My bank account was overdrawn. I didn't do that. I never paid anything late. I was really panicking.

I heard my email chime as I was refreshing my bank account to see if anything had been deposited when I got an email that I had been charged an overdraft fee. Another email came up saying that I had a late fee and needed to pay immediately.

My heart sank.

And then- the sign of all signs happened.

I got an email from my bosses. I opened that email faster than I have ever opened an email in my life. This had to be about the money!

It was here!

It was all paying off!

There will be a bonus!

I will celebrate!

I knew this had to pay off.

Then, I read the email.

They were letting me know that they would be flying out of town for a "much needed" vacation that afternoon and that they would be out of pocket. They trusted that I could handle it and hold down the fort! They knew they didn't have to worry because I would want them to be warm and have a great time! They appreciated me so much! Couldn't do it without me! I am so great!

Wait – What?

They were going on a vacation?

Jetting off to somewhere warm with their kids?

That right there should have been it for me. I should have been out the door. I should have let it all burn down while they were on their warm vacation.

I should mention that it was freezing in Iowa at that time.

I hate the cold.

I was dealing with seasonal depression on top of burn out- while not having any money to live on or even stay current. I already was questioning if this was really worth it. Now- add this email and spontaneous vacation they could suddenly afford to my list of negatives. It was really hard for me to stay positive. I felt like I was being scammed. In fact- I knew I was being scammed. I knew this wasn't right.

I still didn't want to believe it.

Even though I knew- I pushed those thoughts aside. If I did a great job right now- OF COURSE I would be rewarded. They had to pay me. It would be illegal not to, right?

The money had to come. All the hours- all the time away from my life- had to be worth more than this.

When my favorite, now- ex, co-worker - called me and said that she had a job opportunity for me, I was sold before she even told me what it was or what it paid. When she told me that I would be a virtual office assistant again, but this time for one company instead of twelve, I was elated!

It was a window cleaning company in Virginia. I could work from home and have amazing hours!

This was incredible!

I must take a moment of appreciation here, for two things.

One: For my friend that felt such a strong urge to get me out of there that she lit-er-all-y made it happen for me. I could not ever thank her enough for that.

And two: For what had happened at work riiight before I got this call.

There is a good chance that I would have said no had it not happened.

The fact that I quite possibly, would have turned down this incredible opportunity and kept living that layer of lessons for even longer- makes me so grateful that it happened.

My son was graduating second grade. I know that this isn't usually a graduation moment at school. I actually thought that it was one of the weirdest things I had ever heard, but that didn't matter to me. He mattered to me- and he was excited.

They were doing a little program for the parents, and this was my sons first year at his new school. There was no way he was going to be the only kid there without a parent. I had requested it off and gotten the time approved months in advance. I was really looking forward to it.

The minute I took my seat I found him and waved. He had the biggest smile on his face, and he was waving like a maniac. It made my heart swoon. I was so happy to be here. So happy that I didn't forget to request it off. So happy they approved my time off. I was really grateful for everything at that moment.

I felt my phone vibrate. It was a text message from my boss. Followed by another and another and... another.

What the heck was happening? I opened the first text, and the next text and the next.

I was bombarded with threatening messages from my boss. Telling me I had 10 minutes to get back or I would be fired.

Fired.

Right before I left, she told me to have fun, that everyone was so excited for me to get to go and be there for him. That we were so lucky to have a job that allowed us this freedom.

This caught me completely off guard. This is what everyone had warned me about. It hit me like a brick to the face.

And suddenly... - right there in the school auditorium- it felt obvious all along.

I accepted the job offer and said that I could start immediately. I was done. I had enough.

She was so happy for me. I realized that the weight was lifted off of her too. Knowing that I was finally free eased her mind- just as much as it did me.

I worked there with her, for the next 8 years and the beginning was pretty freaking incredible. We built the business up together. We went through some wild, yet hilarious ups and downs.

But that's the thing- we are always meant to grow.

To do more.

And life has a way of forcing us to do more even when we try to stand still.

For a while though, I got to work from home and virtually hang with her all day.

I loved it.

My hours were normal, so I had tons of time with my son. And it was flexible! I was able to be at every event, appointment, sick day, anything that came up for my son, all without any threatening texts! That made us want to work even harder. We were so grateful after what we had been through.

We were crushing it!

Business soared.

I was making decent money and hey- getting paid on time and what I was expecting!? That was enough for me. Being able to pay my bills released so much stress for me. I thought I would be there forever.

Nothing could go wrong.

Our boss even started paying us small bonuses too, with promises that- the bigger we got- the more we would make. We saw that as a huge win. We were finally getting recognized for our hard work! It felt amazing. I was so grateful for the stability that I didn't see anything else.

He started promising us more - but they were never what he said. It was always quite a bit different.

$1000 could mean $25.

But sometimes, $25 was $100.

We never really knew with him. We didn't know until we saw it. But we always saw something.

One Friday, he called me and told me he was going to almost double my salary. I got off that phone call and I cried. I felt such a huge wave of relief. I wouldn't have to struggle anymore.

He promised me we'd talk more on Monday and get it all locked in, but it was guaranteed. He really appreciated me. He saw how hard I was working.

When he called me Monday, I asked when I would start seeing my raise, and he hit me with "oh no, I was just joking around. You know, throwing out ideas- seeing how you would feel about it. Wh- we'll discuss it another time." And he moved right on to what he needed from me for the day.

I sat there, absolutely silent.

I felt sick.

I was devastated.

I saw it all happening again.

I couldn't believe I was back here.

I had to do something to make this all worthwhile. I had to shake it up.

I purchased a new vehicle. It was safe- it was reliable, and I couldn't believe I could afford it. And when I saw it, I fell in love with it. It felt so good. I was so proud of myself for being able to make this purchase.

I felt like it was finally paying off.

I felt gratitude.

It worked.

I felt better.

Then, I saw a beautiful townhouse for rent. I went to see it and fell in love with it too. I could see my son growing up there- playing outside – feeling safe and happy in this home.

I signed the lease right then and there.

Life was good.

Tight- but good.

My boss was always telling me that my raise was coming. He even told me that I should jump on the opportunity to get the townhouse and the new ride! He promised me again that it would happen.

I just had to hold on a little bit longer.

It wouldn't be tight forever.

A few months went by, and everything was a lot more expensive than I realized. The bills at the townhouse were higher than our last place, and somehow, in this city, there were more of them. My car insurance doubled. Everything around me was going up. Everything, but my paycheck that is.

I told my boss that I wanted to discuss my raise. I told him that things were tight, and I really needed to know when this was going to be official.

I needed it to be official.

He responded with "Yes! We do need to talk about my raise!"

I knew it! It was FINALLY HERE!

The struggle was over!

I could breathe!

I had been closing huge deals and I knew I was the number one salesperson and had been for quite some time.

The business was booming.

This had to be my raise.

Then he started talking.

He told me money was tight and he was going to have to cut my hours down temporarily. He really didn't want to, but he didn't know what else to do. I was the last one on, so I was the first one off. It was only fair.

Wait…... what!?

I was barely making it right now, and he was going to cut my hours in half? I couldn't afford my current life if that happened.

That couldn't happen.

I told him that couldn't happen.

It happened anyway.

We moved. I went back to bartending and serving on the side like I always did. I asked my parents for help. I felt like a failure. I felt like the world just kept passing me over. I would never be enough. I felt like I was never going to get out of this pattern of living. I felt hopeless for a bit.

Warmer weather eventually came back around like it always does- and everyone wanted to get on the schedule. The phones were ringing constantly. My boss called me and made me a full-time employee again, but this time- it was different.

I was bitter.

Everything made me mad.

And the icing on the cake?

He cut my salary.

It was because he "had" to. We were just starting back up for the season. We had to recover financially and then he promised me an even bigger raise.

You know- bigger than the one he promised me that I would get- and then he never gave me.

It would be more than I could even dream of because he "took care of his people." He appreciated me so much for taking the hit for the team.

I just had to hang on a little bit longer.

He promised.

I saw every single way that he was taking advantage of everyone this time around. I started connecting how much he did this to us and I saw that I had been aware of a lot of it longer than I realized. The signs were all there and I still didn't do a single thing about it.

Life was really trying to get me to listen,

but I wasn't ready.

I would complain about work to anyone that would let me, but I would never take it to him. Every single day I woke up and was so crushingly aware that this job was killing my soul. The broken promises, the way it made me feel- I had to get out.

Internally, I knew that I was done. But I couldn't think of a single thing that I could do that would make me enough money to live the life I currently had- let alone the one I wanted. And I definitely couldn't think of anything that I would love more than working from home and being with my dogs. I couldn't leave until I figured that out.

But - I didn't know how to figure that out?

So, I did what I always did, and I started bartending. It was on a college campus, which was new for me. With my experience, I immediately became the head bartender and I loved it. I loved the people and the quick advancement. And it wasn't a bar- it was for events. That meant that it wasn't the same regulars every day. That was a positive change for me. Hearing the same drunk stories every single time you work- that gets old fast. But people at events?!

Way better.

They are always having a good time.

It's always new.

It's almost always fun.

One day I was setting up a bar event and I told my boss that I had to get out of my other job. It was killing my soul. I told her how hopeless I felt, and she lit up like the 4th of July.

She needed a new daytime event coordinator and the only reason she didn't ask me was because she knew that I had my other job. She didn't think I would quit working from home but if I was serious- the position was mine.

It was mine if I said yes.

This was a REAL career. This sounded like everything I had ever wanted. I said yes in a heartbeat and the position was officially going to be mine next month.

Everything felt scary, but also- exciting.

Big things were changing.

I could feel it.

I just needed to hang on for a little bit longer.

I was so hopeful during those months. Marco and I had made an extremely rash decision to turn our friendship into the real deal and we jumped in headfirst.

The start of us dating and living together is intertwined. At this point in our relationship, I was feeling great about our quick decision.

We were having so much fun and I was head over heels in love with this guy.

Now I was also getting my dream job and FINALLY leaving behind the job that I had been vowing to get out of for the last 4 years?!

Life was good.

It was finally working out.

February turned to March. Everything was going to start. I was getting ready to submit my two weeks notice. Once that was out of the way, I would get to start my new career! I had already started the training. I was a ball of energy!

I made a soul promise to myself that 2020 was going to be my year. You know the kind of promise you can really feel all the way to your core. After almost 3.5 years of being completely solo, jumping into my new relationship felt incredible. Marco and I also made a vow that 2020 was going to be our year. We were really going to give it our all.

Dream relationship, dream careers.

Life was finally going to be what we wanted.

I had everything I needed.

Nothing could stop us.

I could feel it.

(Deep sigh.)

The one thing, I never knew could happen, happened. A freaking pandemic. A whole entire world pandemic happened. I don't need to tell you. You know.

My position was on hold because -suddenly, there were no events. We couldn't do events. Nobody could even be in the same room together, let alone have a party.

The school even shut down temporarily.

Then, the job I hated, the job that I was so excited to finally leave? I had to hang onto it now. I had to just be grateful that I had a job- AND- a job that I could do from the safety of my home.

That was huge. I was lucky. I would just work hard and do what I could. I wouldn't listen to promises. I would be clear about communicating that I did not want to hear anything about promises. I would do what I needed to so that I could have a positive outlook. So that I could make it. I had to survive in this.

But I could still feel the sinking in my chest.

It felt like I was deflating.

I remember thinking- I am never going to get out of here.

Ever.

I wanted to cry. Why couldn't things just work out? I didn't understand. I was really trying. I had years invested. Why couldn't I ever get ahead?

But I had to shake it off. The world was crazy right now. It was like nothing I had ever seen. It felt like a movie and not in a good way.

I Just needed to try to be grateful as much as I could because I knew that things could be a lot worse. I knew that I was going to be okay.

Work was always slow in the winter. We relied on March to recover financially. I knew we'd be busy. They needed me. I kept reminding myself, that, at least I had a job, right? This became my daily mantra- my routine. Just trying to pretend like I was happy at work. I could push through by being grateful instead of sad. Make the best of what you've got and all that- right? People push through jobs that they hate every day! And hey- at least I am at home!

I took a breath.

(Deep Sigh)

I successfully changed my attitude -the best that I could- and I got to work each day.

Then, I got the call.

Virginia was shutting down. Nobody could go into customers' homes to do the work. Nobody knew what was happening. We weren't essential employees.

We lost our jobs.

The thing that- I thought- I wanted the most, just happened.

I no longer worked at the soul crushing job that I had been DYING to leave for the last four years. The one that I had to hype myself up for- just to be able to step into my office in the morning.

I should be ecstatic! Elated! Full of happiness! I finally got what I was asking for...

but... this? This wasn't what I was picturing.

And now?

Now I was in full panic mode.

I had been working 2-3 jobs since I was legally able to. Even before I was legally able to- I found ways to work. I sold candy bars, I offered to mow, umpired little league games, I even volunteered if it meant a potential job later. Anything. I was always working.

And suddenly- I didn't have a job. I have ALWAYS bartended or served on the side- whenever I got bored or needed extra cash? I have always had access to them.

But now?

The bars were closed.

The restaurants were closed.

My income was gone.

My crutches were gone.

I didn't know what to do. I started thinking logically and realized that the last time I leaned in- really leaned in and listened, it was with Marco. I had been scared out of my mind to date again – but I listened, and we were working out great!

I knew I wanted more of that feeling- so, I did the only thing that I could think of. I leaned into him, into us –and into what I was feeling.

What I found that I was feeling the most took me by surprise.

I just wanted to enjoy it. I didn't want to stress. I'd been stressing about money and my 8 billion jobs my entire life.

I wanted to know what the other side looked like. The calm. I was craving it. I had my fill of chaos. I just wanted some peace.

So, that's what we did. Marco kicked it off by grilling for me during an Iowa winter. It was freezing and this man was grilling us burgers. We were laughing. He had me tucked under his arm while I had him wrapped in a hug. We were really in the moment. Feeling it. Really enjoying being together.

It was good.

Life. Was. Good.

Maybe it all burned down. I didn't know. But in that moment...

I just didn't care.

The event coordinator job would still be there when the events came back. It's not like I didn't have anything.

I just had to hang on a little bit longer.

A few weeks passed and my dream job was still not showing any hope of coming back any time soon. Marco had just been swayed into a new career as an inspector. He was loving it and their office needed a complete revamp. He wanted to know if I had any interest in doing it.

I needed something and, I won't lie. I was nervous all throughout Covid. It made me uncomfortable in a way that I had never felt before and I was really feeling nervous working around people.

When Marco mentioned that I could work from home until my dream job came through- I was hesitant. I didn't want to do the office life anymore. I knew that. But... working from home sounded better than ever. It could be temporary. Just until we knew more about what was happening with this new world we were trying to live in.

We had also become really good friends with Marco's boss and with his wife. When his boss officially came to me with a position that he described as "barely even part time," it was hard to say no. All I had to do was answer a very light phone call volume for him.

The catch was that it could be any time of the day, any day of the week. And - I wouldn't be getting paid hourly. I would only get paid by the phone call, which honestly- didn't seem worth it. Being tied to my phone, *always*?

That sounded stressful.

That felt familiar and not in a good way.

He said that we could just try it out, discuss a small weekly pay if it picked up.

I am exhausted on a soul level as I write about the day that he offered me that position.

I didn't want it.

I knew 110% that I didn't want it.

I said no *three times* before I caved and said yes.

And I immediately followed up with- "well, temporarily."

I didn't want to do this.

I knew that I didn't want to do this.

And I still said yes.

I said yes because I REALLY wanted to help him get his business going. I knew that I could, and I thought- maybe this is the time that I really get to help build something and I will actually get to ride the ride! We will all get paid. Hard work and dedication will have us thriving!

That was all I wanted at my last job. Instead, I just kept watching them ride the wave while I was drowning in the background. I even watched as they used me to stay afloat. I allowed them to drown me.

Well, no more!

We were riding this thing together.

I also said yes because, I'll be honest - I always want more time with Marco. I could never have enough time with that man. I could even go with him to inspections if I wanted. My boss didn't care. I could work from the car. And, if I wasn't riding with the love of my life- I would be at home, safe and sound with my dogs.

This wasn't going to run my life.

I was really going to get to build this up, do something big.

These were our friends.

It would be different this time.

I had a million reasons why I should say "hell yes!"

I had a million reasons to be excited about this incredible opportunity.

But......

My soul was screaming no. I didn't understand why. I just felt a hard hell no every time I thought about answering the phones. That couldn't be my only reason for saying no. I am a dreamer- but I also knew I needed to do something. You can't pay bills on dreams -and all that.

So, I said yes.

I realize now that I said yes mainly because I was scared. I didn't know what else to do and it felt stupid to say no. I felt the financial pressure. I needed to figure out something- and it was a lot harder to figure out than I thought. I wasn't coming up with anything that I would love to do and that I was qualified for.

When I said yes, he gifted me with a MacBook. He couldn't pay me much money while we built the business up, but to show his appreciation- the MacBook was mine. And, of course, there would be money in my near future!

We talked about all of the things that would happen when we took off. We were all vibrating with excitement that night. We celebrated. We started talking about the future. Making plans and I was putting them into action that night.

That MacBook gave me a huge incentive. It made it feel real. I was excited now. My initial feeling had to be wrong. I got a MacBook! That was cool! That was a guarantee to me. It showed that he was for real. He wouldn't make me empty promises. I could relax. This is where I should put my efforts. We will all win together.

I was getting what I always wanted.

Or was I?

I ended up right back at the virtual assistant job. I was always working. I was always on. At first it was so familiar that I fell right back into old habits.

My "barely part-time position" was actually a- "barely can schedule sleep" - situation. I was in charge of everything. I was charge of the office – phones, schedule, payroll, promotions – you know, anything anyone has ever done in an office? That's what I was in charge of.

I was also a personal assistant – therapist - assistant to the accountant and to the lawyer - problem solver-you name it. I was doing it.

I was even helping one of our contractors get their video communication up in their office because we needed them to have it.

But - I was still only making my "barely, part-time" pay. I didn't even realize it at first- but then, one day I had to check our numbers. When I saw that business was BOOMING financially compared to last year, it hit me hard. He still hadn't given me my raise. I decided to take charge and give him a call. I asked him about my raise, and he quickly responded the money wasn't there- but soon! He promised.

But…… the money was there.

I could see it.

Then I thought- well, maybe there is more to business than I am realizing.

Maybe he had more costs this year.

Maybe there is something that I'm not seeing. It'll be there. This has to all pay off.

I know it will.

Then he asked me if I could run some Amazon returns for them. And if I could come pick them up. Oh- and if I had time if I could look up patio furniture for him. He wanted to keep it under 4 grand.

I sat there.

Shocked.

Sad.

Stunned.

I couldn't believe I was back here. This was the same pattern. The same job. Why couldn't I break away from this?

Did I do something to deserve this that I wasn't aware of? I was making $250 a week working every single day of the week and I was never off.

Don't do the math.

It is disgusting.

I must pause here.

I knew.

I knew right then and there. This was EARLY on.

I should have said right then and there- if you cannot pay me- then this is wrong, and I am out.

I should have set boundaries.

Stood up for myself.

I KNEW that this wasn't going to get better.

But instead of doing anything about it- I gave up. I quit.

Not the job I should have quit.

I quit on myself.

I didn't listen, *again*.

I went against my initial feeling, *again*.

I made excuses every single day, just like before.

We were friends and when we made it - we made it together. There must be things that I wasn't seeing.

It would all pay off.

It had to pay off.

He promised.

Listen, I NEEDED this to work out. My hope meter was empty. I was spent. I needed to see a different outcome. I needed someone to prove to me that they would keep their promise for me to believe again.

At this point, the universe had been trying to teach me this lesson for a very long time. I had become more and more aware of this through each and every job that I have had. This was well over a decade of trying to get it through my skull.

I thought I was learning them- but here it was, smacking me in the face again.

I couldn't be wrong again.

How was I wrong again!?

This time it had to make up for all the shit that I had been through.

I was trying so hard.

I was really giving every single job- *everything* I had.

I was trying to level up.

I was doing things that I didn't even think that I could do- and I was killing it.

His business was BOOMING. Everyone was busy. It would all pay off. It had to. This was my friend. He wouldn't burn me. He would show me that my hard work was honestly appreciated- seen. He would restore my faith in humanity, in promises, and in hard work paying off.

All of this couldn't be for nothing.

I was working constantly. I couldn't stop. If I wasn't actually needed for a chunk of time, it felt weird. I felt like I was dropping the ball- missing something. I was thinking about it, checking in on it, anything. There was always so much to do.

My boss would call and text me throughout the day and night about how overwhelmed he was. There was always so much more I could be doing to help him not be so stressed. He wanted me to take on more and more. I did. Without a raise. He promised me though- being less stressed he could focus on the budget. Then I could make more. He'd talk to me next week about the raise. He'd figure it out.

He promised.

Marco and I started arguing- a lot. Not big fights- but we definitely weren't building our relationship and we definitely weren't loving our time together. I feel this so deeply thinking back on this because our time together is so good. I feel connected – loved- excited- everything- every single time I see him. I just love him and our time with all I have. It was really hard on us that our time didn't feel great anymore. I always felt like I was bracing myself because I knew he was going to be upset about something I did or didn't do. I didn't have enough time or mental energy for all of this.

I felt stretched so thin.

But that's just it- our time- wasn't our time. I was always working.

And now, we were fighting.

I was barely even contributing financially. I had to throw things on credit cards because I still wasn't getting paid for all my hours. Marco saw everything. He saw how much money they were spending. He saw how much they were blowing. He saw how much he disrespected me. How moody and often mean he was to me. It was a lot. And to make it worse, he couldn't get through to me. I was blinded by how much I wanted to help grow the business.

I truly thought that Marco was out of line for being so mad and I made excuses for our boss. I picked work over us. I see that now. I wouldn't even listen to him. I couldn't see anything while I was in it.

We talked through it, and we promised to try to be better with our time. We both knew we had to stop fighting.

He meant what he said. Marco being Marco decided to surprise me and texted me to come outside. I heard the rumble of the bike and immediately knew it was him. He had planned a quick little day date.

I melt just thinking about how sweet he is.

I ran upstairs to meet him out front. He pulled up into our driveway on a motorcycle after work. Our boss had said that he could take me out. He wouldn't bother us with work. He told us to go and have some fun. I was so excited to see Marco - really see him. Just get away and be us. But when I ran out front and saw him on the bike- my very first reaction was no.

Which was weird.

Really weird.

I always felt YES when it came to hopping on the back of the bike with Marco. Something felt off. I didn't know what- but I just knew it did.

I immediately shut that thought down. I was not going to ruin this sweet surprise. Especially after how tense we had been. I knew that he went out of his way to surprise me and that he would have a whole plan. We needed this. I wasn't afraid. I just knew that something wasn't normal. I didn't know what. It didn't make sense. Marco is such a safe driver - why would I be worried? When I thought of it like that, I was able to relax. I probably just felt weird about not working.

I never took off.

We were going to have a great time.

I wanted to enjoy it.

Marco was taking me back to where it all began. At the start of our relationship, he had been working out of town about an hour away. We love to go back and appreciate the nights of talking all night on the phone and the dates that we have had there. We love reliving all of our moments. It feels so melty and wonderful to do together.

It was a beautiful day in June for a drive filled with trees, water, and scenery everywhere. Just what we needed. We had our sunnies on- backpack ready- and a few of my fingers slipped into his pockets- leaning in on him like I always do on the bike.

We hit the road.

Marco spontaneously decided to swing into the state park so that we could take a walk and see everything. It was *so pretty*. We walked out to the lookout point where we looked over the water and took it all in. Everything felt so good. So right. I couldn't believe I almost said we shouldn't do this.

We smooched.

We danced.

We talked.

We laughed.

We were really in a state of appreciation. Really taking in our time together. We felt like us again for the first time in months.

It felt really good.

In true Midwest fashion- a few guys walked down, and we started chatting as you do with strangers here. We asked them if they would take a photo for us. They said that they would be more than happy to, and Marco handed his phone to one of them.

He took a few and kept moving around and changing the phone angle. I was thinking -this guy is super dedicated to getting a perfect photo of us. Then he asked us to move over. He said that the light kept hitting us really strangely in the photos. He couldn't get it off of us no matter what he tried. We laughed about it and assured him that it was fine. It was nice. It aligned with our perfect date. We thanked them again and were on our way.

We were only a few minutes away from our taco destination when we left the state park. Marco pointed up at the rocks to show me something. I glanced up but couldn't hear what he was saying so I made a mental note to ask him when we got to the restaurant. I looked back towards the road, and everything was different. There was fresh gravel down and we were too far over. I didn't even understand how we got that far over. We looked away so quickly. The bike hadn't moved. I didn't feel it move.

Why were we so far over?

How were we so far over?

I can't explain what happened next- in any way other than by saying that - this was always supposed to happen. It was always going to happen. I could not learn my lessons. Marco could not learn his lessons.

We needed something drastic.

And that is what we got.

We got something drastic and miraculous.

It was always going to happen.

I know that in my soul.

It needed to happen. The bike started to lose control. I felt Marco brace as much as he could. I felt it- the moment he knew he had to put the bike down. I knew we weren't getting out of this. I knew we were going down. I knew that this might be it. Everything felt like it was in slow motion like in the movies-when, just for a few seconds, you can really see everything clearly. It feels like nothing is moving.

I could see him.

I could see the guard rail.

I could see the train tracks.

The river. The rocks. The road.

I knew- and I was aware that I knew - that this could be the very last moment of my life.

I wasn't afraid at all.

I felt peace.

I took a deep breath of air, and I knew, that no matter what happened next- we were either both okay or we were gone together.

I felt calm in every single part of my body.

I felt weightless.

And then, I was flying.

I flipped over Marco. I didn't even realize I was in the air until my head and shoulder crashed into the earth. I can still hear it.

Everything went black.

We were going 45 MPH.

We were not wearing helmets.

We were not in road gear.

We were surrounded by obstacles.

I blinked my eyes open slowly. I couldn't hear or feel anything. I thought we were dead. I thought it was like Beetlejuice. Marco was standing over me and I could see his lips moving- so I focused on his lips really hard until I could make out what he was saying. I realized he was saying my name.

Once he realized that I was focusing on him and that I was alive- he started saying "my shoe- my shoe" over and over while pacing back and forth. I noticed he was only wearing one of them and then I pulled my focus back to his lips until the sound started coming back and reality started to flood my brain.

I took a moment to really look at him. He looked so scared. I've never seen him like that. He was so worried about me. About everything. I couldn't make sense of anything yet. I just needed to focus on him because, as long as I could see him moving – breathing- talking- walking- I was calm.

We were okay.

I tried to sit up but when I pushed my hand into the ground – my chest hurt. My arm collapsed. I was able shift my body around to get up without using my arms. I slowly stood up and caught my balance after a few wobbles. My head was throbbing. My chest hurt- but I could move my arms. Everything was sore but seemed to be in working order. Then, I immediately thought- we definitely had to be dead because – how were we okay? Nobody is okay after an accident like this.

I looked at Marco in his one shoe and realized that he was in shock and then wondered if I was in shock too. I started joking around, like I do in serious situations, and that helped to rock him out of his shoe trance. We were able to assess the bike and surprisingly- that wasn't too bad either!

I was just so thankful that we were both okay.

We were both together.

I looked at him and I realized no matter what happened- this needs to be my number one. We are my number one. Seeing that look on his face- I realized just how important I truly am to this man. I always knew- but that sealed it in differently for me. It made me really see how much he wants me to win. How much he loves me all the way through- for exactly who I am. We level up together. We build together. And I realized one thing in that moment.

Shit had to change.

I didn't know how- but I just knew, this was it. It had to change. Nothing could ever be the same after this. We found his shoe, my hearing aid, and our phones which were also all miraculously fine. We hopped back on the bike, and we were headed towards home.

Our jackets that were in my backpack probably saved my spine and probably created enough space for me to hit my head but not snap it back.

Marco had gone down with the bike. I realized he had A LOT of road rash. SO much road rash that I wasn't even able to touch him on the ride towards home. I had to keep my grip on the back of the bike. His poor body took a beating. He was bleeding everywhere. There was so much skin torn off and so many pieces of rock and gravel imbedded in his skin.

That first shower was horrendous. I didn't know how we were going to make it through. Listening to him cry out in pain - seeing him in shock, his body shaking in the chair. It was horrendous. That moment is etched into my brain. I will never forget how that felt or the look on his face.

I had tiny rocks in my hand and very minor road rash that I was barely able to manage. I don't know how he got through it. I don't know how he showered. I don't know how he managed the pain of cleaning it out every day and removing the debris from his skin.

That kind of pain is indescribable. You have to live it to know it and I hope you never do. Seeing him go through that I saw something new. I saw incredible strength in him. Strength and determination that I hadn't seen in him before. I realized right then, that as much credit as I give him- it still isn't enough.

I think about that moment a lot. It makes me grateful every single day that it was what it was. Not more- not less. We needed the whole damn thing.

I had a concussion, and I threw up a lot. Almost a year later and I am still dealing with the head trauma- but that's for another time. We were basically okay in the grand scheme of it all. What I really want to talk about is what happened after the accident.

The next few days were weird.

Really weird.

This is why I am here. Why you have this to read. The rest of the story –what happened with the job, the MacBook that they took back from me- how it all unfolded. The details don't even matter here.

All that mattered was that:

I couldn't do that job anymore.

I couldn't do that job ever again.

I couldn't work like I used to.

I couldn't let this kind of work run my life, ever again.

I was done.

I didn't know the lessons yet- but my soul knew that I was done with this chapter.

I should be excited, elated!

But my thoughts were driving me insane!

All the negative things that people had told me about myself – for my entire life – kept flashing through my brain- constantly. I rarely EVER thought about any of this. So, it was weird that I couldn't stop obsessing about the list of things I'd heard over the years.

"I'm too nice, too loud, too much energy- I talk too much. I need too much. I expect too much. I'm too different. I need to just be more like other people. Dreams don't make money. I need to settle down. Everyone has to do things that they don't want to do. You're not easy enough. You're too much work. You're too wild."

That list was long.

I started thinking about all the things that people told me were too much, too little – too weird – too whatever. I looked at everything. And I thought to myself – do I really think that? Did I ever think these things? I couldn't get off it.

I couldn't figure out why I was obsessing over this list. I could have died, and this- this is what I was choosing to think about? It didn't make sense. But I couldn't stop no matter how much I told myself to knock it off.

So, I dove in. I realized, I really wanted to know. Did I agree with these people? Most of whom I don't even associate with anymore? Do I, or did I ever think these things about myself?

I didn't. It turns out that - not only did I not agree - but that list- that list was made up of my favorite things about myself. My absolute FAVORITE. The things that I realized, truly felt like me. This list is all of the things that I was craving for somebody to see- and love about me for a lifetime. I wanted someone to see me so completely- that they would want to pull out even more of these things. Realize that they were what made me……. Me.

I started thinking about this shift in my perspective and it unlocked so many new doors for me. It started with the "you're too much work" comment. I felt really drawn to exploring this.

It ended up leading me to, what I thought- was my biggest childhood trauma. It made sense suddenly. I needed to heal this- and then everything would make sense!

So, I did just that. I dove in 110% and I really started to heal it. I really started to let pieces of it go. I did the work. I was really excited to have that first break through! This was going to be huge!

But then, it wasn't.

I didn't feel better in a big way and suddenly the trauma I had healed, seemed kind of small. If that had such a big place in my life, like I thought, why didn't I feel more of a release.

Looking back now- I know why. I was just getting started! I had barely scratched the surface. But scratching the surface made me realize – I couldn't do this anymore.

I had to become a completely different person.

I had to become who I was when I was a kid.

When I was free.

I had to become who I was always supposed to be.

Life needed me to wake up so that I could wake other people up.

Do what I am here to do.

I need to reach my people.

My energy needs to flow.

I need to listen to myself before anyone else.

I couldn't explain it- but I just knew that I had massive things to do.

I had positive energy to let loose. I needed to find everything that fills me with happiness so that I can inspire others. I needed to fill my hope meter back up so that I could help fill it for others.

I am here to show everyone that you have all of the tools that you need to shake the shit out of your life and get what you really want. What you really deserve. What you really need. And when I fill that hope for others, it spills over.

Positivity seeps out all over the world.

Others inspire others.

It is the best kind of domino effect.

The things that the accident taught me are priceless. Amongst many things- these are the lessons that I feel are the most helpful to others and have proven to be a great place to start, for myself.

*Things that kill your soul aren't worth it.

If it isn't something that an attitude adjustment can shake- it is your body telling you it's time for something new. We are not here to work at things we hate and die. However- don't diminish your past. You needed every single thing that has happened for this next part.

There are lessons in everything.

Lessons come in all shapes and sizes. The sooner we can take our discomfort and lean into it and learn to not let it run over us- the sooner we can move through it. Let yourself feel it- and then let yourself heal it.

Don't make excuses.

Take responsibility for your part in where you are and then ask yourself – what do you need to shift? What do you need to get out of it?

*Journal about it- talk about it- anything! Explore!

Get curious about yourself.

Do you see any patterns in your life?

Do you want anything to be different?

Why?

What will it look like if you achieve your wildest dreams?

Why can't you have them?

What can you do to get closer to it?

Ask yourself anything that feels good.

The more you learn about yourself- the faster you progress.

The more fun your life gets because it fills up with more of what you genuinely want!

Life does not have to be the same situation, the same kind of people over and over again.

Learn from your life and use it.

*"You cannot pay your bills on promises."

My father in-law said this to me, and he was 100,000% right. Never again will I do anything based on the promise of something else. If it doesn't feel good to say yes, I am saying no. I am not saying that there will never be promises made to me- but I will never say yes to anything BECAUSE of a promise- or a guaranteed.

I've had a lot of guarantees – not be guaranteed. You don't know what will happen from one moment to the next. When people start talking promises- I immediately shut that down. I want day to day action. I don't need the words.

People really do show you who they are. Believe them. Stop assuming you know them better than their actions. You don't.

*A Job is Just a Job.

There will ALWAYS be some job to do just because you have to- or think you have to- or you want to.

And somethings won't look anything like you thought they would.

If you want something- you have to get it.

You have to try new things and lean into whatever is pulling at you, whether it makes sense or not.

You have to trust that you know you - better than you realize, and that life is leading the way.

Every new path leads us somewhere we need to be at that very moment in time.

The more you learn to listen and hone in on your instinct- the more you your life feels.

The more peace you find.

***People will use you if you allow them to.**

You literally set them up to do so. By never saying no- by jumping when they say jump- by taking on too many tasks- without speaking up or saying no.

Saying yes to quickly without checking in with yourself.

Not standing up for yourself- allowing moody – mind games- that is on us.

That is on us for playing back- for not speaking up- for saying yes when we want to say no.

For thinking it's the only way.

Codependent tendencies are for us to break.

We give too much power to other people over our emotions.

As long as someone else has power over the way that you feel- your life won't feel like your own.

*IT. IS. NOT. THE. OTHER. PERSONS. FAULT.

This one was a tough pill to swallow. This happened to me again and again. Job after job. Relationship after relationship.

The minute I took responsibility in the way that I allowed people to treat me, I was able to let it go.

I was responsible for myself, and I didn't take care of me. I put myself last, always. If I'm not even important to myself, why would I expect anyone else to feel that I was? We can still be flexible- but the situation should be serving you. It should feel good to you.

The people that I have lost along the way all taught me lessons through our relationships. They helped me find my personal power. They helped me find more me. They showed me that it's okay to go separate ways.

That is where we find growth and make space for new things.

There doesn't have to be any negative feelings towards each other. It doesn't have to be hurtful. We all make mistakes. We are all learning. You can just let each other go.

When we are angry- resentful- full of negative feelings towards a person, a situation, anything- we are not in a healthy space. It doesn't help us.

In accepting the lessons- learning- and letting go - you make peace with yourself. You forgive them and you forgive you.

When you make peace with yourself, you make peace with everyone.

Everything starts to heal.

Everything feels manageable. Everything feels more fun.

Even when it's messy- you know that all of these little things, they are what make the big things so big, so grand and you know- it all comes together in the end.

When you know- you know.

You know what you need. You know when you need it. You know when it's time to shift and you know when you are doing something that is holding you back.

Even when you don't realize it in the moment.

Letting fear run our lives- that extends the lesson. Maybe you are having a blast with it- maybe you love this lesson! Or, maybe, you are ready for something new. Maybe you know you need more. It doesn't matter what stage you are at in your self-development journey.

Doing more things that you love- slowing down and savoring your experiences- finding more ways to connect with yourself. Those things, at any stage in your life -at any lesson in your life- will bring your more of what you love.

They will enhance your experiences!

They will make you more aware.

Those things are never bad. Those things lead us to our tools. And our tools?

Our tools will lead us to our favorite selves.

Filled with more of what you need. More of what the world needs. More of what you want.

And the lessons, those will just keep coming until you receive it and can move on to the next. This means that you are truly choosing what happens next. Do you stay put- or move forward?

While there is no right or wrong answer, I can tell you this. If you feel as hopeless as I did- as unhappy, then- lean in. Trust yourself. Listen to your initial feeling and just get curious. Find out what you really know because at least when you are learning- life gets a little bit better each time.

I can hold space for everyone's happiness instead of everyone's sadness.

This.

This is my favorite lesson that came from this. I FINALLY received this lesson through the loss of friendship with our boss and his family. It finally got through to me. At that time -they had a lot of traumas, too. I felt for them on such a deep level, but I also couldn't hold their pain. I couldn't make excuses for them. I could empathize and I could understand- but then I had to move on.

That was for them to work on. Not me.

That is what I should have done- but I didn't. I wasn't in a healthy space, either. I didn't know how to set a boundary to save my life. I didn't know how to help them, and I didn't know how to separate myself. I didn't know how to prioritize my relationships.

I didn't know A LOT of things that I know now.

I tried hard to hold their pain for them. I tried to love it out of them. I tried to help it out of them. I threw myself into wanting to fix everything for them. I exhausted myself and let myself down by expecting so much. By putting so much on myself. I treated them like they were broken instead of showing them how to find their tools- because- I didn't even know how to find mine yet!

Finally receiving this lesson was what made me throw myself into becoming a life and health coach. Something that I have wanted since I can remember- but was always too afraid to go for.

I had to be able to do this differently.

That experience- and everything that built it- that all brought me here.

Every single thing had to happen how it did.

The more I lean into that theory - the faster things happen. The more I move.

Everything will continue to happen exactly how it is supposed to. The more you relax and trust that you know what's right and wrong for you – the more of your life you get. You can spend an entire lifetime fighting it- not receiving it and never find what you truly want, or – you can make it happen.

You can demand your life.

I've connected other times that I would hold pain for others- and realized that me wanting to fix everything for everyone- does nothing good. It wore me out energetically. I did a lot of assuming what people were feeling, and then I would take on those feelings. It didn't matter if they were true or not.

That was what I knew that they felt.

That wasn't always the case- but I couldn't see that.

I cared too much.

Yes, you can care too much.

How do I know? Because that brought me a lot of pain- physical, emotional, mental. I started to resent them for making me feel this way and they were resenting me too. It came off like I knew them better than they even knew themselves- and, if I knew so much – then, why weren't they better?

Then- Poof!

We are out of each other's lives and full of resentment. When we would think about each other- it was full of negative energy. Grief, sadness, anger, blame. It's all there. And it's a waste of energy. It shouldn't be this way.

I carried that with me for years with multiple relationships that had ended. I would lash out with my words whenever they were mentioned, and then immediately drown in guilt for saying it, wishing I could take it back. It was an endless cycle of negative emotions and pretty soon- it felt like I was drowning in them.

That's when I realized- it's me that I had to shake the shit out of. It's me making it this way- giving away my power. It's me that is forcing these relationships, this life. It is me that is in the way.

So, I flipped the script. I did the opposite of what I had been doing and I chose positive instead.

Nothing meant for you will miss you.

It was time to relax.

When you hold happiness for people– they feel that. When they are low- they feel better around you because you see them, and you let them be. You encourage their journeys for exactly who they are showing you that they are. You don't need them to be perfect- because they do not affect you. You know that they have their own journey to figure out and it is not your responsibility.

That gives people the freedom to fly. You have faith in their story. It doesn't matter what happens next. That is on them. You are both free when you hold happiness for others. Even when they aren't. Even when it's messy. You know that- once they find the lesson, there is a next part- and you can't wait to see everything unfold!

It's exciting!

And it's so cool because in taking care of yourself- it rubs off on others. The people closest to you, they start to shift too. Sometimes, without even realizing it. Your happiness and the happiness you hold- that can't be hidden. You physically feel it when you are around it and that is absolutely beautiful. Everyone can use more of that.

What you see is what you get with me. I have a lot of these short stories. Jam packed with lessons that I have finally figured out a way to share. Each day I find more of my purpose- my passion and that is to reach my soul people. The people who can take my story and run with it. Use it to shake the shit out of their own selves and go get the life that they really want.

It all starts with awareness.

The more aware you are- the more you grow because once you know- you can't unknow it.

Pay attention to where your attention falls.

It's important- no matter what it looks like.

If this is hitting you hard in the feels right about

now-

You are not alone.

I see you.

I feel you.

You are right where you need to be.

Breathe.

Well, hello again!

You might have realized that this book- was kind of weird, like me! No chapters- weird spacing- weird ways of wording things.

That is all intentional.

I have spent a lifetime trying to write the way that I was told I had to in order to be successful, and that? That wasn't working for me.

I have made it my life's mission to help others find themselves – bring their light to the world, their uniqueness, their weird.

This is part of mine.

Chapters make it harder for me to read sometimes because I feel like I can't get invested and stop halfway through.

So, I quit reading before I am ready.

So, I said- goodbye to chapters.

I mean, why not?

Let's try it out.

Life is too short to be anything other than wonderful. <3

Thank you so much for reading this and encouraging me to be more me, as well.

If you loved this- if it sparked- TELL ME!

Seriously.

I would love to know what resonated with you.

Please feel free to leave a review with a lesson that you have learned!

We can use this space to share our stories and spread positivity.

We can help each other find our way through.

You might also be wondering about the name-

Just Bree.

You know that point- right before you meet someone- and you ask for a quick rundown about who they are?

Well, when people would ask about me- everyone would stumble on their words and then say- I don't know – it's just Bree.

You'll see.

To me- that has always been one of the best things about me.

So, I'm being more of that. Just Bree.

It's all about building from this point on.

We are riding this thing together.

That is, as you know- all I have ever wanted.

I appreciate you more than you know. <3

-Just Bree.

P.S. If you loved the book- go to JustBreeHLC.com to see the picture. If that isn't a sign- I don't know what is.

Find your patterns - switch it up! Change your life. ♥

Get curious instead of sad - defeated - whatever you feel that doesn't build - FLIP YOUR SCRIPT! Get curious. Why do you keep ending up here? What have you experienced? Feel it. Appreciate your strength - your compassion - Everything.

Learn more about yourself - find your peace - find your way through. Everything good will follow + amplify. ♥

Just Bree

JustBreeHLC.com